The Lucky Penny Guru Presents

The Penny Auction Guide

- QuiBids Edition -

Written by A. Hartley

for my muses: Madison, Maisie and Murphy

with special thanks to my family and friends for all of their support

Table of Contents:

Section 1 – Introduction...9

Section 2 – The Basics..15

Section 3 – Auction Tips...27

Section 4 – Bidding Styles..35

Section 5 – Conclusion...47

Section 1: Introduction

Why a Guide on Penny Auctions?

In many ways, penny auctions have replaced eBay in the discount shopping realm. Since more and more people are looking for new ways to buy things at a discounted price, this Guide was created to help the novice penny auction participant get started on the right track. This guide will help teach you the ropes of how to approach a penny auction site and what to do to win using the least amount of bids possible. Taking this approach will also save you the most amount of money possible!

This Guide specifically focuses on QuiBids.com because that is the website that I'm the most familiar with at this time. Though the strategies and tips outlined here will be helpful in all other penny auction sites, you will want to familiarize yourself with the specific rules and tools of each site before applying all of the knowledge contained within this guide. Not to mention you'll need to research the website to make sure it's not a scam. Some of them are, so you need to be careful.

Is QuiBids.com a Scam?

A lot of people out there believe QuiBids is a scam. This perception is understandable as penny auction websites in general have received plenty of bad press. And yes, there are good sites, and there are bad sites out there on the Web. This is why it's important to do your research before putting down any money and giving anyone your personal information! Before you even ask, I can't give you a list of all the good websites or all the bad ones. All I can do is tell you that I have had success using **QuiBids.com.

So no, I don't believe QuiBids is a scam. And yes I know a lot of people will tell you otherwise. But if you read through the bad reviews you'll notice a common trend. There's a lot of people who didn't know what they were doing before they jumped in head first. It's kind of like what would happen if someone gave me the keys to a motorcycle. I've never even been on a motorcycle nor do I know what you do to get it to start or even move forward. If I plopped onto the bike and put the keys in expecting to go somewhere, I'd be disappointed when I found out I couldn't even turn it on!

So how do you avoid jumping in head first? Well, buying this guide was a great first step. But now you have to read it, in its entirety. You have to learn how QuiBids works, what you can do to maximize your bids and then you have to watch some auctions without bidding. After you do all that, then you're ready to start using QuiBids effectively.

My Own Penny Auction Story

For those of you wondering if I am affiliated with QuiBids, I'm not nor have I ever been. I'm just an average person who learned how to use the site and won some pretty cool stuff. You see, it all started on my last birthday when I decided to purchase the promo bid pack (100 bids). But before I jumped in and started bidding I spent a good amount of time reading reviews and the QuiBids 101 section of the website. Though it is important to point out that in all my research, I somehow managed to pass over QuiBids 3 auction winning limits in a 24 hour period. So the first night, I won a 15 bids voucher, a small crock-pot and a $10 gift card to Walmart + 10 bids voucher. I went to bed that night thinking it was cool but not really thrilled with what I had won.

The following night I won a Storage Jar Set for $.20 (20 cents) that retails for $100. I spent $15.99 on shipping and used 6 bids, which cost $3.60, all totaled up I spent $19.80 on the jars. At this point, I was considering myself very lucky. Even with the cost of my initial bid pack and shipping, I was ahead for what the cost of the jars were retail. I was ecstatic! I had used 9 bids for everything I won so far, and had 116 bids left (That's 100 starting bids + 25 voucher bids total – 9 bids used in storage jar auction = 116 left). At this point, I decided I needed to do some more research. So I Googled "QuiBids tips and tricks" and found a lot of great and some not so great information. Then I did what one of the tipsters suggested and watched some auctions before bidding again. It was then that I realized that while there was no science to winning auctions, there were significant factors that could make winning easier.

One thing in particular I noticed was how many people were bidding on the various large 55" LCD and 3D TVs. I also noticed that there was a smaller 37" LCD TV that only had 8 people bidding on it. So I watched the auction for a while and then jumped in when the conditions looked right. And within 14 bids, it was mine. At this point, I was doing a jig! And why not? I had just won myself a TV for next to nothing! With the price of the initial bid pack, plus the cost of shipping for the items I mentioned above, in addition to the total cost of the TV, I spent a collective $145.93 for over $900 worth of merchandise!

At this point, I considered myself lucky, and I went back to the auctions to see what else I could win. Almost immediately, I was involved in a bidding war and promptly lost over 40 bids without winning a thing. I couldn't understand why I had won the TV and yet couldn't win anything else. Due to the loss, I decided not to bid anymore. Instead, I watched several auctions as a spectator. During my downtime, I even noticed a couple of iPads go for under $10! But I needed to follow what was going on and not get wrapped up in another bidding war with someone who had more bids than me. I learned how important staying logical was and realized how dangerous it was to be emotionally tied to any 1 item. Because when you're emotionally tied to it, you can't think clearly and then don't watch for signs that you can't win. So once again, I walked away from the computer for a while.

When I returned, I spent a significant amount of time watching the progress of auctions before jumping in again. I focused on one auction and finally won my iPad for $23.10. I also won a $50 Target gift card + 25 voucher bids, and a Microsoft mouse. At this point, I had spent under $200 for over $1500 worth of stuff all in just a week! I felt very lucky! Now that I've been using QuiBids for a while, I can tell you that there is certainly some luck involved, but it's not all luck. You've got to be informed as well and know what to expect. That's why I've decided to share my secrets with each of you.

Why Do I Share My Secrets?

I've decided to share my secrets for two reasons. First, if I spend all my time on QuiBids, then I'll be at my computer all day and not get anything else done around the house. Second, because there are winning limits. I can only win 3 auctions in a 24 hour period, and I can only win up to 12 auctions in a month. While this seems like a lot of chances to win, it really isn't. So with my free time waiting around to be able to bid again, I decided, I might as well try to help others out there. Thus, I get to be productive, and you get a great deal using the techniques I've picked up.

Section 2: The Basics

What is QuiBids?

So what is QuiBids anyway? QuiBids is a penny auction website. You join the site by paying money for bids and then you can bid on different auctions. The price of the auction item is then determined by how many bids is placed on that item. For each bid placed the auction price goes up $.01. Hence the name "penny auction."

The goal of a penny auction is to be the last person to bid before the timer gets to zero. Sounds easy at first, until you realize that the timer resets every time someone bids. The time increments of the timers are 10, 15 or 20 seconds. Each auction has a set timer, which is displayed on the auction page, so you know what is going on.

Auction Timer

So how do you win an auction? You win an auction when you're the last bidder, and the timer doesn't reset itself. Wait the timer resets itself? But why does the auction timer reset itself? Because it's like bidding at a real auction when the auctioneer says going, going, gone! This gives other bidders a chance to bid before the auction closes. So when the counter gets down to zero, you win. But until then, the auction timer just resets back to 10, 15 or 20 seconds and continues counting down until someone else bids and it resets again.

All auctions start out with a 20 second timer. As the auction progresses, at a random interval, the timer goes down to 15 seconds and then 10. If you 'mouse over' the timer symbol next to the current auction price, a text bubble appears that tells you at what price the auction will go down to a lower timer. There appears to be no rhyme nor reason as to why a certain auction item lowers at a certain price. So don't expect any consistency here.

Keep in mind that every time someone bids the price of the auction goes up a penny. This is especially important if you're bidding on a larger item but can't really afford it. I've seen TVs and computers go for over $300. So there's no use in wasting your bids on something you can't afford.

What Items Can You Win on QuiBids?

There is a variety of items on QuiBids that you can win. From TVs to vacuum cleaners and sunglasses, there is sure to be something that interests everyone. Also, remember that this is all brand new factory sealed stuff, too. Most popular items are available on QuiBids, not to mention that there is a ton of gift cards, as well. These gift cards are from various places ranging in value from $10 to $200 and are for places like Lowe's and Home Depot, Staples, iTunes, department stores, restaurants and much more.

Bids

How much do the bids cost? The bids are $.60 each, and they are purchased in bid packs. The sizes of the bid packs vary, depending on how many you want to buy. But your initial bid pack when you first sign up is 100 bids for $60. After that if you're still learning the site, I'd suggest buying into a smaller bid pack at first. The smallest bid pack is the "Baby Bid Pack" which provides 45 bids and costs $27.00. The largest bid pack is the Ultimate Bid Pack of 800 bids for $480.

Here is the break down list of all the sizes and prices:
Baby Bid Pack is 45 bids and costs $27.
Beginner Bid Pack is 75 bids and costs $45.
Promo Bid Pack is 100 bids and costs $60.
Standard Bid Pack is 300 bids and costs $180.
Premium Bid Pack is 600 bids and costs $360.
Ultimate Bid Pack is 800 bids and costs $480.

How Does QuiBids Make Money?

So how does QuiBids make a profit if auction items only go up by a penny per bid? QuiBids is profitable because of the money they make off of all the bids. They don't make money on the auction item, rather with the auction itself. Since the auction price goes up $.01 for every bid placed on that item and QuiBids charges $.60 a bid, they can make a huge profit on popular items. To show you how much money QuiBids can make on an auction I'll use the examples of the 37" LG LCD TV and 16GB Wifi + 3G iPad I won.

I bid 14 times on the TV before I won it, which means I spent $8.40 on bids (14 x $.60=$8.40). The auction price was $30.24 and shipping $29.99 for a total of $60.23, plus the bids I used is $68.63 total. Not bad considering retail on the TV is $799! Yay me, I got a killer deal on a TV.

QuiBids made out pretty well too, since $30.24 is a lot of pennies which equal a lot of bids. 3024 of them to be exact. So 3024 bids x $.60/bid = $1814.40. That's a lot of money. If we take the $1814.40 - $799 (retail cost of TV) = 1015.40 in profit. ($1045.64 counting the auction price)

Now I did a little better on the iPad that I won. I only bid 9 times, which means I spent $5.40 to play. The auction price was $23.10 and shipping $12.99 for a total of $36.09, plus bid's equals $41.49 total. Not bad considering retail is $569.99.

QuiBids did nicely as well with 2310 bids x $.60/bid = $1386. $1386 - 569.99 = $816.01 in profit. ($839.11 counting the auction price)

My experiences on winning those auctions aren't always the case though. Sometimes you have to spend a lot more in order to win the auction. This happened in another iPad auction I participated in, but left after only a few bids were placed. When I went back later on to check the stats, I found out that the 32GB Wifi iPad sold for $77.20 and the winner used 629 bids. In this case, the retail cost of the iPad was $499 and the price of the bids used was $377.40. When you add the cost of the bids to the price the winner paid for the auction item, it was only $44.40 under the cost of retail. Which is still a good deal, however, it's nowhere near the $77.20 the item "went for" in auction price.

Retail Price

In the example above, I'm willing to bet that the person who won was ready to pay full retail for the item. So what this means is that if you're bidding that many bids for a single item, you have to be willing to pay full retail for that item. If you have purchased a large bid pack, you might as well bid on an item you really want and can still afford to purchase. That way if you don't win, you can still get the value of the bids you spent off the price of the object with the "Buy It Now" option. And like everything else you purchase in life, be aware that the retail price on QuiBids may not be the lowest price you would pay for the item if you shopped around. Then again it won't be the most expensive either. Typically QuiBids charges the manufacturers suggested retail price or MSRP.

Buy It Now

So what is the Buy It Now option? It's like the "buy it now" button found on many eBay auctions. If you lose the auction, you can purchase the item for retail price. In the case of the iPad listed above, if that bidder had lost, the Buy it Now option would have been a good choice. Because then that person would get to apply the bids he/she spent trying to win the item towards the retail cost of it. The iPad would still be $499, but there would be a bid rebate of $377.40, leaving the remainder of $121.60 to purchase the iPad.

You only have 2 hours to purchase an item you lost an auction on. So make sure you are prepared to buy an item before bidding on it. If that is your intention, I suggest purchasing directly after the auction ends. That way you don't forget. I lost an auction on a gift card and immediately got involved in another auction. Before I knew it, my time had expired, and I felt like I lost out on that item twice.

QuiBids as a Discount Site

If you're in the market for a new computer, TV or iPad, you might want to consider using QuiBids as a discount site. This statement doesn't mean you will necessarily get a significant discount. But if you focus your bids on 1 single auction of that item, and you don't win the item at a discounted price, you can apply the money you spent on all the bids in that auction on the item itself with the buy it now button. So best case scenario you make a screaming deal.

Worst-case scenario, you get the item you were already intending on purchasing at retail price.

If this is what you are intending to do, it's still a good idea to do the research first. Don't just jump in figuring that you are going to buy the product anyway. When I was first starting out using QuiBids, I did this with a Sony CyberShot digital camera. Because I was planning on buying that specific model anyway and it came up for auction one day, I figured I had nothing to lose. I spent no time researching it and just jumped right into the auction. After spending over $150 in bids, I still had not won the auction. So I used the Buy it Now button and purchased it at full retail price. I didn't lose any money, since I was able to apply the price of the bids towards the camera, but I probably could have done better had I handled this differently. The next day, three of those same cameras sold for under $5.00 and the most any of the participants spent on bids were $50. Even though, you're planning on buying the item anyways, it's a good idea to do the research first. Specifically, I should have researched when the best times of the week and day are to get that item at a better deal.

Even though there's a section of this guide that focuses on research, later on. Let's take a quick minute and go over what 2 things I should have done before bidding on the camera.

1.) I should have followed the camera auctions for at least a few days to find out what the trends were: when the auctions sold for the least amount, what time of the day and what day of the week.

2.) I should have used my Auction Tracking Sheet to help me keep track of what was going on. This way if there is a trend of cameras selling for less around midnight, then I would know that auctions happening around midnight are worth checking out.

Keep in mind that this is not a surefire way to get a good deal. Because what you don't know, is what other auctions were going on at that time that the item you're interested in sold. Maybe those other cameras were such a great deal during those other times because there were many larger item auctions (TV's, iMac's, iPad's, etc) going on. And on the day I bid it was the highest dollar item, or the only camera item being auctioned off. This can have a huge impact as to how many people are bidding on that item. Some people don't care what they are bidding on, as long as it is one of the higher dollar amount items available. And other people don't care what type of camera they win as long as they win one.

Real Bids VS Voucher Bids

Getting credit towards the item you've bid on, for the Buy It Now button, is only doable when using Real Bids. Using the earlier example in the Buy It Now section, had the person who purchased the iPad used "Voucher" Bids, they would not have been able to apply the cost of those bids to the price of the iPad. Voucher Bids are bids that are won in auctions or given out as a result of winning badges and they have no cash value towards buy it now items.

Speaking of Badges

Badges are awarded for hitting certain achievements, and they come with free bids. For example, you get a badge for placing your 100th bid. You also get a badge and free bids on your birthday. And badges are also shown with your user name, and last auction won to other bidders during an auction.

Winning Limits

Another thing to keep in mind is that QuiBids has winning limits. You can only win up 3 auctions per 24 hour period. In addition to that, when you win an item valued over $285 in value you have to wait 28 days to bid on another of that exact same item. For example if you win an iPad 16GB Wifi + 3G, you can't bid on another one for 28 days. One thing you could do, however, is bid on an iPad 16GB Wifi, because it is not the exact same item. One runs on a 3G network and the other one, Wifi.

Also, you can only win 12 auctions total in a 28 day period, and only one of those items can be over $999 in value. QuiBids puts limits on the higher-priced items to try and ensure that everyone is getting a chance towards the big items. You can bid on a Limit Buster though. Limit Buster's take your total auctions for the month down by 1 or 4 items. Winning a Limit Buster will allow you to bid more for the month, but they will not allow you to win more than 3 items per day. Also, Bid Voucher auctions don't count towards your monthly limit, but they do count towards your daily limit.

One last thing to mention on the subject of winning limits is that if you are a person who is bidding on multiple auctions at 1 time using the "bidomatic" feature, you can only be winning 5 auctions at one time.

How to Bid

There are two different ways to bid. You can be what is called a single bidder or you can be a bidomatic bidder. A single bidder is someone who bids, one bid at a time. This is done by using the big green Bid button on the auction page. After someone uses the Bid button, it shows up in the bid history with the person whose bid user name and the word single after it. However, if the person is using the bidomatic tool the auction will say bidomatic after the user name instead of single.

Bidomatic Tool

So what is the bidomatic tool and how do you use it? The bidomatic tool is used to place any number of bids between 3 and 25. It will place the amount of bids for you, up till you win the auction or run out of bidomatic bids. Once the bidomatic tool runs out of bids, you can reset it to start all over. It is a versatile tool because it allows you do other stuff without keeping glued to the computer screen. It was developed to allow you to bid when you weren't directly in front of the computer. For example, it will continue bidding for you if you have to run to the restroom or let the dogs out.

The tool can also be used to bid on an auction when it reaches a certain dollar amount. However, using the bidomatic tool does not guarantee you a win. But will help you to participate in an auction that is occurring at an odd time. For example, say you want to bid on an auction of a Kitchen Aid Mixer, but you don't want to wake up at 4am to do so. You can decide that you want the bidomatic tool to bid up to 25 bids for you. You simply put in what dollar amount the item has reached when you want the bidding to begin at. Though you need to keep in mind, that once you are out of the maximum 25 bids it will not keep going, unless you are there to reset it.

Familiarize Yourself with the Site Before Bidding

I can't stress enough the importance of being familiar with the QuiBids site before bidding. I've talked to friends who have bid on auction items from the home page, instead of going into the individual auction page, because they didn't realize that clicking on an auction listing would bring more information about that item. They had no idea they were doing it wrong and had so much more information within their grasp. Both of them promptly lost a lot of bids by not being prepared.

So, please before bidding spend some time looking around the QuiBids site. Go to the QuiBids 101 tab on the website, and read the information available to you. Check out the My QuiBids tab, examine the bar at the bottom of the screen that has your watchlist as well as how many bids you have left and account info. There are a lot of tools that make it easier for you to succeed should you take the time to look into them.

Another reason to familiarize yourself with the site before bidding is because the QuiBids site is not static. They are continually updating their site to make bidding fair for everyone, and certain tips and tricks may not be as effective as they were at the time I'm writing this guide.

Research, how do you do it?

After you've registered and gotten your account set up, go to the home page. It will show you some popular auctions happening right now, but those aren't the only ones. This is something you will find out if you follow my very first tip of getting to know the site before bidding! At the bottom of those popular auctions, there is a link that says "View All Auctions." This will take you to a longer list of all the current auctions as well as some of the ones that are upcoming. This is a good place to start looking. It will show you what items are available or coming up. It can also give you ideas for what you want to try for if you don't already have a specific auction item in mind.

If you know what you want, click the "Add Auction to Watchlist" text that shows up under the item on the list of "View All Auctions" page. This way if there are multiple auctions for that one item you can keep them all in your list. On the View All Auctions page there is a search bar where you can type in the item that you are interested in. For example, let's say you're looking for a KitchenAid mixer. Type KitchenAid in the box and it will bring you to all the upcoming auctions within the next 24 hours. It will also provide you with a list of all the past KitchenAid's that sold in the last week or so. This is a very helpful tool if you are compiling research. With this, you can see the end times and end price of all auctions from the last week. If you click on a specific one, it will take you to the actual winning auction page. I like to look here, because I like to see how many bids the person who won, spent. This is helpful because if there is a trend of a high amount of bids, I know that I better not bid on this item unless I am willing to pay retail. It also will let me know how popular this item is, especially if all the auctions sold for a higher dollar amount and all bidders used a lot of bids.

Now that you know the two main ways to gather your research, either by following the live auctions or by looking up the auction history you are now ready to use the included Auction Tracking Sheet found at the end of this guide. This sheet will help you keep track of the auctions and look for trends. While no auction follows a norm, you will, at the very least get an idea about how a particular auction could go down by filling out a sheet on each item you want to bid on. You may also be able to get an idea of how often the auction item your interested in, is available. Once you have done this research you are ready to start bidding, but now you are an *informed* bidder and not just jumping in head first!

What Time of Day is the Best to Bid?

There really is no definitive best time to bid. I've read that the best time is between 12am – 4am Eastern time, but I don't agree completely with this myself. There does seem to be less traffic at that time, but there are also fewer prizes. This is why I recommend doing your research before bidding on a specific item. It will help give you a starting point and an idea of the amount of bids that may be required to win that object.

Where to Start

Start small. QuiBids will start you out on beginner auctions when you first get going. These basically are auctions you can win with little to no competition. This gives you a very small taste of what is to come. On your first auction choose a gift card valued at $10 or $15 or a voucher for 15 bids. Because, these types of auctions will have the least amount of competition. And don't forget to try out the below tips. Just because they are low competition, doesn't mean they will be a cake walk!

Once you've mastered the low-competition auctions, then it's time to move up to auctions that are slightly more competitive. I'd stick to anything in the $25-50 range. I know you are itching to win something cool and might want to try out for that iPad or iPod Touch, but this would not be prudent. Instead, how about going for an iPod Shuffle? As this is a more realistic goal. Or maybe a gift card for iTunes? You will have more luck with these items than the big items previously mentioned. And just because they are low competition does not mean you don't have to do your research first! You've got to be wise if you want to get ahead on QuiBids!

Section 3: Auction Tips

QuiBids Tips – Tips To Help Keep You From Wasting Unnecessary Bids

Be Prepared By Following These Tips:

1.) Get to know the site before you start playing. Read the tips posted by QuiBids, as well as user comments. Explore every nook and cranny. Look at what auctions are coming up as well as past auctions. Watch several different auctions just to understand how quickly or slowly things can move. Having a better idea how things happen will increase your chances of winning something you want.

2.) Don't jump right in. You won't win an auction you don't watch a while before you start bidding. Get to know who the bidders are. Penny auctions are as much psychological as they are luck based. So watch the auction and try to analyze the behavior of the top bidders. I've found, that the auctions I've won the most have been because I spent a few minutes watching what is happening before bidding. And yes I have seen auctions close before I got a chance to bid, and while that is frustrating, it's better than wasting bids on an auction you can't win.

3.) Spend at least a week filling out the Auction Tracking Sheet. Be informed by researching the item you want to buy. Find out what it sold for and how much. If there is a trend of that item selling for a certain price at a certain time, then you can look for auctions coming up around that time. This will not guarantee you win the auction, but it will give you an idea of what to expect and help you set your expectations realistically.

Example: Recently I did this with a camera bag I wanted to buy. After a little research, I found that the auctions happening around 2:00PM were selling for the least expensive at around $2.00 (remember less $ equals less competition at that time). So I waited until another auction was scheduled for that time and won it for $2.47. Because it is more of a specialty product (being a fashion /professional camera bag) there weren't as many people bidding on it during the day, when there are many more much higher value item auctions going on. During the evening hours of 11pm-midnight, the camera bag was selling for much more at $12-15. Because at night there aren't as many high value items up for auction and it became the focus of the other participants.

Tips about the Bidomatic:

1.) Don't bid in an auction that has multiple bidomatic bidders and more than 10 people if you have less than 100 bids. Whenever possible, watch those bidders and let them use up each other's bids first. Especially, if there are more than 2 bidomatic bidders going back and forth with each other. Because if you've got less than 100 bids, you could go through them in 5 minutes and wouldn't win a thing.

2.) Use the bidomatic tool to automatically bid for you, if you aren't going to be around your computer. If you've done your research, and you've found a trend that an item you want sells around a certain time around a certain price, but you won't be around your computer. Test your skills and set the bidomatic tool. Don't set it to start on an even number though. Try setting it to bid at $12.37 instead of $12.00 or $12.50. This way you are less likely to have set your tool at the same time as someone else. Keep in mind, you can only set up to 25 bids and that you won't be watching the bidding to make sure the conditions are ideal. But sometimes you can get lucky!

3.) Set your bidomatic tool for 3 bids (which is the minimum you can set). Then let those 3 bids be used up. If there appears to be a lot of interest in the auction, you can pull back after your bids have been used. Then after a minute or so reset the bidomatic tool for 3 more bids. Use your judgment for when you think it is safe not to bid, but do it often enough that it doesn't look as if you've left the auction. This is a good tip to help conserve bids, and still play by QuiBids new rules. *(**The new rules are**: you can only request the bidomatic tool to start bidding if there are more than 2 seconds left on the count down timer. QuiBids also restricts the amount of times that you can activate and deactivate the bidomatic tool.)* Since you are letting your 3 bids be used, you don't have to worry about QuiBids penalizing you for deactivating the bidomatic tool too often.

Using this tip, I won the iPad. This tip is especially helpful when bidding on an item that already has 1 person using the bidomatic tool and 1 or 2 single bidders actively competing against each other. If you get lucky, the other bidomatic bidder has to reset their bidomatic tool or just decides to move on to another auction because you won't quit. And the single bidders decide to wait and let the other bidomatic person out bid you and then you win!

Don't expect the moon and the stars. These tips will help you adjust your expectations:

1.) Have realistic expectations. Don't expect to win the big items right away or with a small bid pack. You will not win a flat screen TV or computer on your first bid. You just won't. Start with smaller items, like gift cards or items valued under $40. Because there won't be as many people bidding on them and usually people don't spend a lot of bids on these items.

2.) Be patient. Expect to sit at your computer for hours watching the little timer count down from 20 seconds or less. You will not win in the first 10 minutes, especially if it is a higher priced item. I spent a couple of hours playing and watching the iPad auction before winning. And I have spent many hours just watching and playing other auctions. In order to be successful you must have patience, and be able to spend the time watching the site.

3.) The more people that are bidding the more bids you will need to win, and the higher the price of the item will climb. If you are looking to jump into an auction, only start bidding when the number of bidders has dropped down to 8 or less. If it's a high traffic auction, you never know when someone will jump in. By starting out with less competition, you will have better odds of winning. If the number of bidders increases dramatically, you may need to take a step back for a while and wait it out.

4.) Typically speaking you must have a presence in the auction before you can win. You will need to bid a few times before the other bidders take you seriously. I've never won an auction on my first bid.

Know your limits, follow these tips to be careful with your money:

1.) Only purchase bids if you can afford to spend the money. Don't assume that you will win something and make that money back.

2.) Set a budget for how many bids you are willing to lose for an object. For example, if you are bidding on an item worth under $15, it wouldn't make sense to spend over that amount in bids.

3.) Be aware of the full cost of an item before bidding on it. Recently I found an auction that appeared ripe for the picking. I took a few moments and watched it end, but I did not bid on it. The 55" TV was going for over $500, and while I thought I could win it, I knew I did not need another TV and could not afford the hefty price tag.

4.) Expect to spend as much as 500 or 600 bids on an auction of an item that retails for $500 or more. In this case, I would have it be an item you were already planning on purchasing. This way if you don't win, you can apply your bids to the purchase price. You can win an auction for fewer bids making it a better deal, but if you don't expect it you won't be disappointed if it doesn't happen.

Use logic, rather than emotions when bidding. The following tips will help you keep a cool head:

1.) Leave your emotions out of the auction. If you let your emotions get the best of you, you'll lose the auction and tons of bids. If you think, "come on, I really want this item" and then don't pay attention to what the other bidders are doing, you'll lose big. You have to go into an auction with the right expectations to have any chance of winning it. So just because you really want a 55" inch LCD TV does not mean you will win it. Odds are there are other people out there with more bids to play with than you, that also "really want" that item.

2.) If you aren't having any luck, and you are getting frustrated. . .walk away from your computer. It just turned emotional, and you are going to waste bids. I'd suggest quitting for the day and doing more research before coming back.

3.) When an auction ends right after you've quit bidding, don't assume you would have won if only you placed 1 more bid. Especially if you were in a bidding war with someone. Odds are you would have just lost more bids because you don't know how far the other person was willing to go, or if someone else would have jumped right in. It is frustrating to see an auction end after you've given up on it, but focusing on how close you could have been will only cost you more bids in the next auction.

Don't forget that timing makes a difference by follow these tips:

1.) It's all about timing. Some people will tell you the best time to bid on QuiBids is between 12am - 4am Eastern time. While that can be true, also consider that there are fewer items available during that time of the day, as well. The best thing to do is to look around at how many bidders are involved in various auctions, specifically the ones that you want to win. If the auctions have 15-25 people or more per auction, then it's a busy time of day. And, depending on what items you're looking for, you might want to wait until it slows down.

2.) Watch an auction you are interested in from the beginning. Don't bid on it from the beginning, but watch it. This way you know who the players are and can start to determine when a good time to start bidding is.

3.) Continue watching the amount of bidders and competition throughout the whole auction. If traffic seems to pick up, and bidders are being more competitive it might be time to take a step back for a few minutes. This way you don't lose unnecessary bids.

4.) Focus on 1 item at a time. Some people bid on multiple items at once or bounce back and forth between different items. It will increase your odds of winning if you have patience and can focus on just 1 item at a time.

5.) Once you've been playing for a while and have some wins under your belt, look for an item that may not be as popular as the big items. When I won my 37" TV, there were 4 larger TV's up for auction and the bulk of the bidders were trying to win them. When I won my iPad, there were 2 other iPads, 2 iMac computers and a couple of TV's also available to bid on.

Section 4: Bidding Styles & Strategies

Bidding styles, tips and ideal auctions to use them

There are 3 styles of bidders: impersonal, defensive and offensive. It is helpful to know the different styles so that you can tell what kind of a bidder you are, as well as, know what you are up against. I have provided a description of each bidder type as well as an ideal auction setting to use that style in and helpful tips. One important note, is that these ideal auction settings are based on auctions I actually won, using that bidding style. Different styles work for different people, different auctions as well as different times of the day. For example, you may find being an impersonal bidder works for high value items, while for me, it works best for items under $30. While these styles are a great place to start you may end up using them as a guideline to help you develop your own bidding strategies.

The impersonal bidder: best for auction items valued under $30 or auctions with fewer than 5 bidders

If you are bidding on an item under $30 or participating in an auction with fewer than 5 bidders, one method I've found that is effective is being an impersonal bidder. Impersonal bidders don't appear as if they are pushing the buttons of the other bidders. They place their bids in the middle of the count down. For example if the timer is for 10 seconds, an impersonal bidder will place their bids when the timer hits 5 seconds. This way they are not bidding directly after someone else or bidding at the last second. I find this method works for me, on lower priced items the best. Not to say that it won't work on larger ones but that the circumstances have to be perfect for it work on any auctions that have a lot of bidders attention. Specifically popular or high valued items.

This method works because it helps to dissuade new bidders from staying in the auction as well as doesn't provide enough stimulus for bidders who take a more offensive bidding style. It is kind of like the tortoise and the hare fable. An impersonal bidder is the tortoise who's slow and steady wins the race. It should also be said that, it may take 10 or more bids minimum to win.

The ideal auction situation for this is when everyone else is being last second or defensive bidders. Ideally there is at most 1 bidomatic bidder, and the rest are single bidders. When the timer gets down to 1 and resets, if there have been a couple of single bidders, bidding after the bidomatic bidders timer hits 1 second, then it is the perfect time to jump in with impersonal bids. Either the group of single bidders or the bidomatic person will bid and then you'll want to wait for the timer to get back down to half before bidding again. Then you repeat the process until you've won the auction or spent your set amount of bids for that auction item.

This approach works for a couple of reasons. First of all, no one likes to feel like their bid was wasted. After a few times of the same single bidders feeling like they are "throwing away" bids by bidding at the exact same time, some of them will hold off before bidding again. This is the point in time that you can actually win the auction. If you've timed it just right, the bidomatic person will pull back or run out of bids, and then no one bids and you get to walk away the winner.

This method also works because you aren't making the auction interesting. You're basically showing them that you are slow, steady and will not get into a bidding war or leave the auction. This will keep the offensive bidder from having any fun and likely make them move on to another auction. This method can work for higher priced items, but because bidders go into the higher priced items expecting to use more bids, the situation has to be just right for it to work.

Impersonal Bidding Example:

I used this style to win a Hype purse that retails for over $300. I watched the auction from the beginning and then started bidding when there had only been 5 people in the last 5 minutes. There was one offensive bidder who had been bidding since the very beginning of the auction, but he/she started to slow down. I took this as a signal of them either getting bored or running out of bids. So I decided to try the interpersonal approach. I bid every time the counter got to 10 seconds (the auction timer was 20). And my patience paid off, it only took 15 bids until I won. The key to being a successful impersonal bidder, is in being consistent.

A few tips on successful impersonal bidding:

1.) Remember slow and steady wins the race, which is why it is important not to get into a bidding war. If someone starts out bidding right after you bid, pull back. Either watch the auction for a while or adopt a defensive or offensive bidding strategy.

2.) Timing is important, don't waste bids if the other bidders are not waiting for the timer to get down to one or two seconds before bidding.

3.) Don't bid against another impersonal bidder. You are both patient and will try to wait each other out, thus resulting in a slow bidding war.

4.) With the exception of brand new auctions, I've had better luck with impersonal bidding on auctions that have had *5 or fewer bidders in the last 5 minutes.*

The Defensive bidder: best for higher priced items

One method that may work on higher priced items is being the defensive bidder. If I was bidding on a higher priced item, and my research told me that there is no real average on auction ending price, I would use defensive bidding. I would start watching the auction around the dollar amount an auction at a similar time went for (since there is no average price, looking at similar timed auctions is your best bet), and then I would go from there. Because, as a defensive bidder, I would be watching the auction and bidding only when it looked like others weren't going to. That way I wouldn't go through my bids as quickly.

Defensive bidders usually only bid when the auction timer gets down to 1 second. Working in this manner will help to make sure the auction doesn't end and may give you the chance to wait out the bigger players as they shoot through their bid packs. I find that it can help to level the playing field when you are working with smaller bid packs.

Defensive bidding auction example:

If I've done the research and I find an item I want to purchase that sells at a much lower price between specific hours of the day, I then start watching that same product in an auction from the very beginning. When the initial rush of bidders to the new auction has slowed down, I activate the bidomatic tool, but only for 3 bids just to have my name on the board.

I do this by waiting until 2 seconds are left on the clock and then activate the bidomatic tool and watch to see my 3 bids run out. Then I repeat as necessary. After some time, I notice the bidders are slowing down with their bidding activity. Hopefully these bidders have run through the bulk of what they were going to spend on this item. When there are less than 8 bidders in the last 5 minutes, and only one of them have been "bidomatic bidders", I start to get more serious. If one of the bidomatic users has resorted to bidding one bid at a time and there are only 1 or 2 single users, I then start using the bidomatic tool myself. But I actually use it the way it was intended to be used, setting it for 6 bids. This establishes that I am not leaving the auction, and I'm a potential threat. Then I go back to only setting the tool for 3 bids at a time and only use it when the timer gets down to 2 seconds. I continue working this way until no one bids, and I've won the auction. This is the exact scenario that took place when I won the iPad.

Keep in mind this is the *ideal* auction. In my scenario with the iPad, no new bidders came into the auction during the course of my strategy attempt. Had new bidders come into the auction, it may have had a very different outcome. And since you cannot control the other people in the auction, it is important to remind you that people are unpredictable. Therefore, this auction technique will not work for all auctions. But it does work well for some!

Here is the screenshot from the iPad auction:

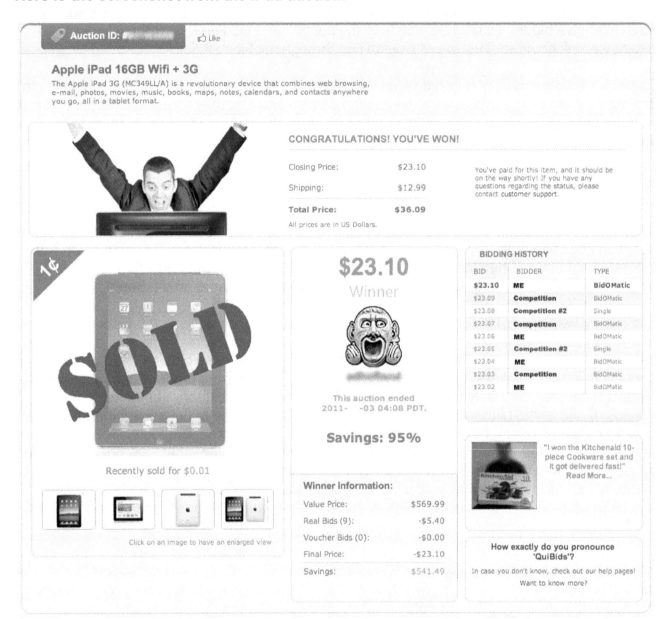

A few tips for successful defensive bidding:

1.) Only bid in auctions with 1 or less bidomatic bidders that have a total of at most 8 bidders in the last 5 minutes.

2.) Use the bidomatic tool to your advantage by waiting until 2 seconds are left on the timer and then only setting it for 3 bids at a time. This is a better approach than activating and deactivating the bidomatic tool. Because doing so will get you penalized and QuiBids will not let you reset your bidomatic tool for a short period of time. This way, you've set it for the minimum amount of bids, and if it appears like the other participants are still too active you haven't wasted a lot of bids.

Please note: You don't want to wait too long to set the bidomatic tool, because as soon as the timer hits 1 second it won't be accepted. If this does happen and you think quick, you can always hit the bid button as a single bidder. That way you won't risk losing the auction because no one else outbid the last person. This means you actually have to watch the auction, and you can't just set the bidomatic tool and walk away. But it is a good way to maximize your bids.

As stated above, this is how I won the iPad. This tip is especially helpful when bidding on an item that already has 1 person using the bidomatic tool and 1 or 2 single bidders. If you get lucky, the bidomatic bidder has to reset their bidomatic tool or just decides to move on to another auction because you won't quit. And then the single bidders decide to wait and let the other bidomatic person out bid you. But in reality no one does, and you win.

3.) Stay away from auctions that don't have a bidomatic tool, unless there is less than just a few people bidding. You don't have the safety net of the bidomatic tool and can throw away a lot of bids quickly if there is too much competition.

4.) Don't bid on an item if the single bidders don't let the counter get down to 1 or 2 seconds. Even if, there are no bidomatic bidders, this type of bidder is hard to beat, unless you let them run out of bids first.

5.) Don't get involved in an auction if the timer gets down to 1 second, resets and there are more than 5 people bidding at one time. With a lot of bidders involved in the auction, it is harder to win. In this case, you may need to watch the item awhile longer until things slow down a little. Use the impersonal bidding strategy in this situation.

The offensive bidder - can work in any situation

The offensive bidder does not have a specific auction type because this strategy seems to work in both lower and higher priced item auctions. This strategy can also work either in the very beginning of an auction or after an auction has been going on for some time. The offensive bidder either uses the bidomatic tool for a long period of time waiting out other bidders or bids directly after every other bidder. Both of these approaches can work because they discourage some bidders from staying in any given auction. Typically speaking, an offensive bidder has a large amount of bids to spend right out of the gate and has no problem using these bids in a bully-like fashion.

If you are watching an auction and offensive bidders, are going back and forth, it is a good idea to just step back from the auction to let them duke it out. When it slows down a bit, and the other offensive bidders have left, then you are safe to get back into the auction. Otherwise, you could lose a lot of bids to stay in that hostile environment. While it is time-consuming to wait out an offensive bidder, it may be well worth it in the long run. Especially if, the other offensive bidder has more bids than you do.

If you are trying out the tactic of offensive bidder yourself, I suggest trying this early in a new auction or after an auction has been going on for some time. If you are an offensive bidder in the beginning, you may be able to keep new bidders and newbies out of the auction, thus keeping the participants to a lower number. Towards the end of an auction, you may be able to cause the bidders that have been in the auction for a while to run out of bids. If this is the case, you could win the auction.

The offensive bidding style can work for both bidomatic auctions and single bidder auctions. Here, is an example I have used for each:

In a bidomatic auction: It worked on a Vulcan Phantom Speaker, with only 10 bids!
In this auction, I started off using offensive bidding directly after every new bid was placed by the other bidders. My goal was to make sure my name was the one that showed up for the longest on the timer. Once the other players started bidding less often and waiting until the timer got down to 1 or 2 seconds left, I set my bidomatic tool for 10 bids. I won the auction after only 4 bidomatic bids. This method worked for me because no new bidders joined the auction and none of the others were playing offensively.

Here is the screenshot from that auction:

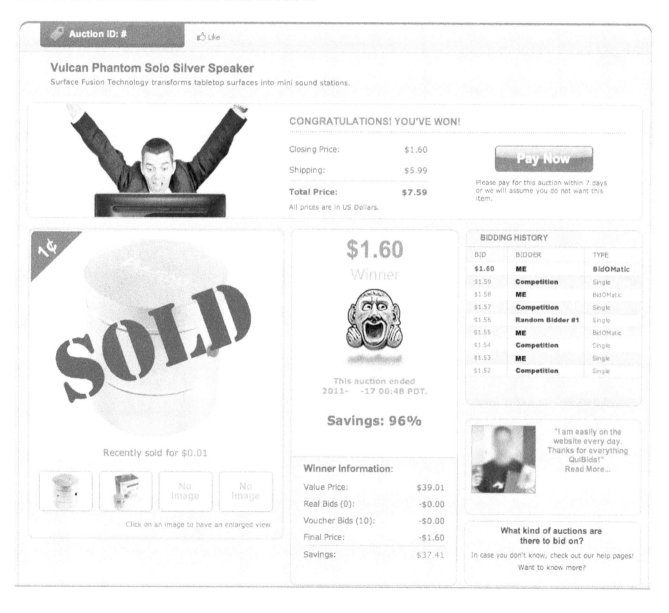

In a single bidder auction: It worked on a KitchenAid Blender, with only 4 bids!

In this auction, I stuck to being a bully. I watched the auction from the beginning and started bidding when the bidders were waiting until the timer got down to 1 second to bid. There didn't seem to be any dominate players who's name showed more often than another. At this point, there were only 4 bidders in the last 5 minutes, and I bid directly after each new bid. Because there was such low competition on this item, I won the auction in only 4 bids! And with shipping and bid price I ended up paying a little over $13 for a blender that retails at around $100!

Here is the screenshot from that auction:

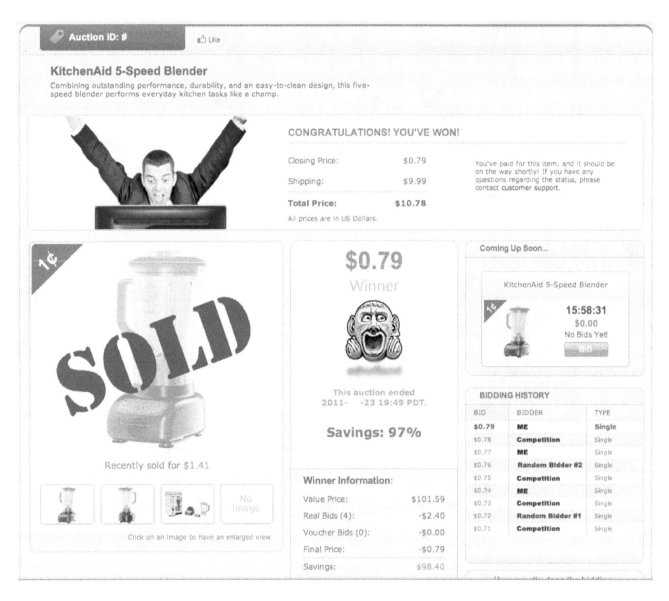

A few tips for successful Offensive Bidding:

1.) Have a large bid pack. You are going to need to spend bids like you mean it!

2.) Only bid on things you are prepared to purchase if you don't win the auction. Offensive bidding can use up a lot of bids.

3.) On lower valued items get into the auction early. Sometimes you can discourage new bidders from joining in.

4.) Set bidding limits on items you don't plan on purchasing if you lose the auction. This will help keep your losses at a minimum.

5.) When using the single bidder option as an offensive bidder, don't let other bidders have any time on the timer. *Bid right after them*. If the bidders in the auction are new or low on bids, this may cause them to leave the auction. **Note**: only do this if are planning on purchasing the item or set a limit to the number of bids you use.

Don't forget the following!

No matter which bidding style you decide to use, *always do your research first!* You might have noticed that this has been mentioned more than a few times. Well, there's a very good reason for this! Research is a very important part of winning at penny auctions. Research similar items, look for trends, view past auction results, and how many bids were used by the winner. This is especially helpful if you are looking to purchase a larger item. As I've stated above, *expect to pay retail*, and you will never be disappointed when participating in penny auctions.

So, how many bids should you expect to use on certain items? Bigger-ticket items like iPod Touch(s) and netbooks, I'd expect to use a minimum of 150+ bids. TVs and more expensive laptops and computers, 300 or 400+ bids. But the only way you will have a better idea as to how many bids to start with is to *do the research and see what the same item has gone for recently*. I'd expect to pay at minimum the average number of bids. There will be cases where items have sold for pennies, and there will be the ones where the winner only saved 5%. But if you do the research you will be able to get a sense of what to expect.

Section 5: Conclusion & Take Aways

Revisiting QuiBids - as a Discount Site

The best way to utilize the QuiBids site is to use it for discount shopping. If you purchase a bid pack with the intention of bidding on just one item that you are already shopping for, *you can't lose*. Because you were already planning on purchasing the item, losing the auction won't mean you lose your money. *You can apply the price of those bids towards the cost of the item* with the "Buy It Now" button. Using QuiBids as discount site is also a great way to get to learn different bidding styles and strategies, because when you aren't as concerned with losing money, you can be "freer" with your bids. Just make sure to only use your bids on 1 specific auction and keep in mind that the price of voucher bids (bids won in an auction) do not go towards the total purchase price if you use the buy it now option.

Know Your Limit

Is it possible to become addicted to penny auctions? Heck yes! Penny auctions may be considered entertainment shopping, but they are *similar* to gambling. Make sure you follow the advice outlined in this guide and know your limit. Remember this point: unless you are going into an auction with the intent to "Buy It Now" at retail price if you don't win, you need to make sure you are only spending money you can afford on bids. Remember that bids cost money and for each bid you place, you are spending sixty cents! This can add up very quickly, especially if you get into a bidding war with another participant. *This is why I recommend only bidding on things you need and being prepared to spend retail on that item.* Otherwise, you could spend a lot of money trying to win things you don't need and might not even be able to afford. It's also why I suggest participating with a clear limit as to how many bids you are going to spend on specific items as well as per day. But remember, even with all of this you will need to *hold yourself to those limits* to make sure you don't get in over your head.

Also, keep in mind that you have to pay a shipping or handling fee for *every item* you win. So you will need to calculate that cost in with the price you won the auction for, to make sure you can actually afford it. A lot of times people only think about the price of the bids and forget about the price of an item should you win it. And don't forget to be mindful of how much money you spent to buy bids in the first place, especially if you are considering buying more bids. QuiBids has a limit for the amount of auctions you can win per 24 hour period, but they do not have limits on how many bids you can buy. Which means you need to be responsible and know your limit.

And be mindful that linking a credit card to your account makes it easier to buy bids. This is good because it gives you a quick option to purchase more bids when you are running low and in the middle of an auction. But it is also bad because you don't have to think about whether or not you should really be buying more bids and spending more bids on any one item. If you are planning on purchasing the item anyways, then it's no big deal. But if you are just looking around and thought you could get a good deal on something you may or may not need, it could get very expensive, very quickly.

Use the Auction Winning Sheet

To help you know your limit, I have created the Auction Winning Sheet and it is located at the end of this guide. It is a great worksheet that allows you to track your won auctions. I personally use it to make sure I haven't gone over my spending budget. A lot of people only pay attention to the money they are spending at the end of the auction itself, and do not take into account shipping and price of bids that was spent. But by filling out the Auction Winning Sheet you'll be aware of everything you've won, as well as everything you've spent.

Not to mention how great of a deal you received on the item you won because I've even included columns for retail price and your savings. I've provided a blank Auction Winning Sheet as well as an example that has the info on the products I've actually won. I included my first 12, so you could get an idea of what the sheet will look like filled out and so that you can see how some items were easier to win than others, and how some were better deals than others. Keep in mind that the items I won had been researched before I began bidding and that I did spend more money on bids, than just what is listed on the Auction Winning Sheet. While the sheet is not designed to track all of the bid packs you have purchased you may want to add them to the list, so you can keep a running tally of everything you've spent.

<u>Recap of important information:</u>

There are three very important pieces of information that I hope you take with you before bidding on QuiBids or any penny auction site.

First of all if you **use QuiBids as a discount site** and plan on purchasing any item you bid on at retail price, *you will never lose*.

Second, no matter what you are bidding on, **do the research first**.

And lastly, **know your limits**.

If you follow these three pieces of information, you'll get the most out of QuiBids and likely get some great deals on auction items. I can tell you from experience that QuiBids is a great site, but only if you know what you are getting yourself into and take the time to learn the system. This way you'll be a success story and not another one of those lazy reviewers who complained about not winning anything when they jumped in head first without even looking.

Read my guide, do your research, and you'll find yourself a well informed penny auctioneer!

Auction Sheets and Examples

Auction Tracking Sheet

Item: _____

Date:	Day of Week:	End Time:	Auction Price:	# Bids Used by Winner:	# of Auctions that Day:

Auction Tracking Sheet – Example Sheet

Item: iPad

Date:	Day of Week:	End Time:	Auction Price:	# Bids Used by Winner:	# of Auctions that Day:
4/8	Friday	5:24PM	$68.64	140	2
4/8	Friday	9:22PM	$88.18	190	2
4/9	Saturday	5:17PM	$13.82	19	3
4/9	Saturday	6:09PM	$73.47	713	3
4/9	Saturday	9:18PM	$81.61	306	3
4/10	Sunday	3:49AM	$195.92	583	5
4/10	Sunday	2:14PM	$52.14	136	5
4/10	Sunday	5:01PM	$61.30	643	5
4/10	Sunday	10:16PM	$93.44	158	5
4/10	Sunday	11:02PM	$83.76	644	5
4/11	Monday	4:36PM	$7.41	67	3
4/11	Monday	7:20PM	$76.82	370	3
4/11	Monday	7:51PM	$55.79	286	3
4/12	Tuesday	11:01AM	$264.13	190	4
4/12	Tuesday	3:41PM	$14.03	13	4
4/12	Tuesday	6:23PM	$114.45	673	4
4/12	Tuesday	7:57PM	$88.21	93	4

I only partly filled this sheet out for an example, if I were really planning on bidding on another iPad I would watch the auctions for a minimum of a week. The longer you watch the auctions, the better chance you have of finding trends. What you can gather from this bit of research, though, is that most of the iPad's went for over 600 bids. Which means that if you were going to try for an iPad you should be ready to buy it at retail and only take part in 1 auction. That way you can make sure you aren't throwing away bids.

Auction Winning Sheet

Use this form to track your winnings and figure out how much you saved!

Won Item	Auction Price	Shipping Price	# of Bids	Bids Price	Total Price	Retail Price	Total Savings

Example Auction Winning Sheet - This sheet tracks my first 12 auctions

Use this form to track your winnings and figure out how much you saved!

Won Item	Auction Price	Shipping Price	# of Bids	Bids Price	Total Price	Retail Price	Savings
Apple TV	$12.15	$11.99	# 20	$12.00	$36.14	$98.98	**$62.84**
KitchenAid Blender	$.79	$9.99	# 4	$2.40	$13.18	$101.59	**$88.41**
Hype Mandin-Double Oversized Hobo	$1.81	$9.99	# 15	$9.00	$20.80	$350.00	**$329.20**
Kalorik Grill w/Radio and iPod Connection	$9.82	$19.99	# 17	$10.20	$40.01	$166.90	**$126.89**
Vulcan Speaker	$1.60	$5.99	# 10	$6.00	$13.59	$39.01	**$25.42**
$15 Lowes GC & 20 Voucher Bids	$.46	$1.99	# 5	$3.00	$5.45	$27.00	**$21.55**
$25 Lowes GC & 20 Voucher Bids	$.35	$1.99	# 8	$4.80	$7.14	$37.00	**$29.86**
Kelly Moore Leather Camera Bag	$2.47	$15.00	# 23	$13.80	$31.27	$159.99	**$128.72**
Apple 16GB iPad Wifi	$23.10	$12.99	# 9	$5.40	$41.49	$569.99	**$528.50**
Microsoft Arc Mouse	$3.90	$6.99	# 11	$6.60	$17.49	$51.45	**$33.96**
$50 Target GC & 25 Voucher Bids	$11.89	$1.99	# 4	$2.40	$16.28	$65.00	**$48.72**
LG 37" LCD TV	$30.24	$29.99	# 14	$8.40	$68.63	$799	**$730.37**
Bodum Presso Jar Set	$.20	$15.99	# 6	$3.60	$19.79	$100	**$80.21**
$10 Walmart GC & 10 Voucher Bids	$.01	$1.99	# 1	$.60	$2.60	$16.00	**$13.40**
Rival Little Dipper Crock Pot	$.01	$6.99	# 1	$.60	$7.60	$15.07	**$7.47**

Notes: